Martin Storey's
afghan knits

Martin Storey's
afghan knits

18 contemporary designs
using Rowan yarns

PHOTOGRAPHY BY
Steven Wooster

BERRY & CO

Martin Storey's Afghan Knits
First published in 2016 by Berry & Co (Publishing) Ltd
47 Crewys Road
Childs Hill
London NW2 2AU

Design: Anne Wilson
Pattern writing (and knitting): Martin Storey
Pattern editing/checking: Lisa Richardson
Charts: Anne Wilson
Diagrams: Ed Berry
Styling: Susan Berry

British Library Cataloguing in Publication Data
A catalogue record of this book is available
from the British Library.

ISBN 978-0-9927968-4-6

Printed in China

contents

introduction

One of the reasons I love designing and knitting Afghans is the wonderful flexibility they offer: because the patterns are so straightforward, you can go to town on a great range of textured stitches or brilliant colourways, or a combination of the two. Another good reason is that projects composed of Afghan squares or strips are so portable: you can knit on trains, boats and planes, in your lunch break or on the beach, your knitting project fitting conveniently into a small bag. For knitting addicts, what could be more enticing and for novice knitters what could be simpler?

My aim in this book is to provide designs with a contemporary twist: the kind of projects that add personality or a touch of glamour to an otherwise relatively plain décor. I have included some, like the creative cables throw, that provide knitters with some stitch patterns to get their teeth into while others, like the beach stripes blanket and mat, are easy enough for novice knitters to manage with ease.

I hope very much that you will use my designs in this book as a starting point for experimenting with your own combinations of stitch and colour or even of scale. Nothing could be simpler than to turn them into a much bigger throw, for example, or perhaps a bedside rug, by choosing a thicker yarn and bigger needles.

Those of you already familiar with Rowan yarns will know I have recently been creating designs for two 'knitalong' Afghan blankets, and I have been surprised and pleased to find how popular the project has been.

I hope you have as much knitting the projects in this book as I have had in designing them.

colour blocks blanket

Knitted in garter stitch in four toning colourways of Rowan *Felted Tweed* (or *Pure Wool Superwash Worsted*) this blanket is made up of 63 squares – 20 plain ones, 12 with a dark blue border and pale grey centre, and 31 with a pale grey border and mid-blue centre. Each square is cleverly worked by the k2tog and k3tog decreases (the diagonal lines seen in each square), then the final square is formed by joining together the row-end edges. Pattern on page 46.

colour blocks cushion

Made from similar squares to the
Colour Blocks blanket on page
8, and in the same yarns, this
design consists of 9 squares, with
the central square the only plain
square, and 4 of the remaining 8
squares with a dark green border
and grey centre, and the remaining
4 with a grey border and brown
centre. Pattern on page 48.

creative cables throw

This throw is a treat for anyone who loves knitting cables, as it comprises six different cable patterns, in seven different colourways, knitted in Rowan *Pure Wool Superwash Worsted*. Pattern on page 50.

simply stripes cushion

This lovely toning cushion is created from 12 squares of an interestingly textured garter stitch ridged design, with each square employing a stone coloured stripe with another colourway, all knitted in Rowan *Felted Tweed*. Pattern on page 56.

simply stripes blanket

This is a larger version of the Simply Stripes cushion, using 63 squares (9 deep and 7 wide). The flecked Rowan *Felted Tweed* yarn creates a lovely tonal yet bright design, which helps to add texture and colour to a simple sofa. Pattern on page 56.

wintry blanket

This features two lovely chunky cable designs in Rowan *Big Wool* offset by narrower cable stripes, made in three strips. It would make a great end-of-bed throw if you increased the length. Pattern on page 59.

winter trees cushion

Another very pretty lacy design, using two different lace motifs, knitted in either Rowan *Alpaca Colour* with its natural soft striping or in *Felted Tweed* or *Pure Wool Superwash DK*. As with the Springtime cushion (see page 32), the lacy motifs are centred in a square edged with garter stitch. Pattern on page 62.

little folk cushion

This charming little cushion employs nine different motifs knitted in two colours only in either Rowan *Wool Cotton 4 ply* or *Summerlite 4 ply* making it relatively simple to work. Four geometric motifs combine with a little rabbit, bee, heart and elephant that would look great in a child's nursery too. Pattern on page 66.

little folk blanket

And here are the same nine motifs as the cushion (see page 22), knitted in the same yarns, but this time joined together to form a cot blanket: 7 squares long by 6 squares wide, finished with a narrow contrasting garter trim. Pattern on page 70.

modern art blanket

Knitted in Rowan *Pure Wool Worsted* garter stitch in five differently
coloured strips, this very simple blanket is also very effective. You can
choose from this version in seven colours or a more monochrome version
in six colours (overleaf). Pattern on page 72.

icelandic cushion

And this cushion is a similar treat for those who like knitting colourwork designs! And, with just two colours in a row, and two different designs, it is simpler to knit than it looks. Knitted in Rowan *Felted Tweed Aran*. Pattern on page 74.

springtime cushion

This is ideal for those who want a little lacy project that is relatively easy to work. With its 'hearts and flowers' design, it requires five 'flowers' and four 'hearts' blocks to complete the cushion top. Each block is knitted in stocking stitch with a narrow garter stitch border. Knitted in Rowan *Summerlite 4ply*. Pattern on page 80.

springtime blanket

A larger version of the cushion (see page 32), it requires 63 squares to be made – 32 'flowers' and 31 'hearts'. You could, if you wished, translate this design into a light summer wrap by making it longer and narrower. Knitted in Rowan *Summerlite 4ply*. Pattern on page 76.

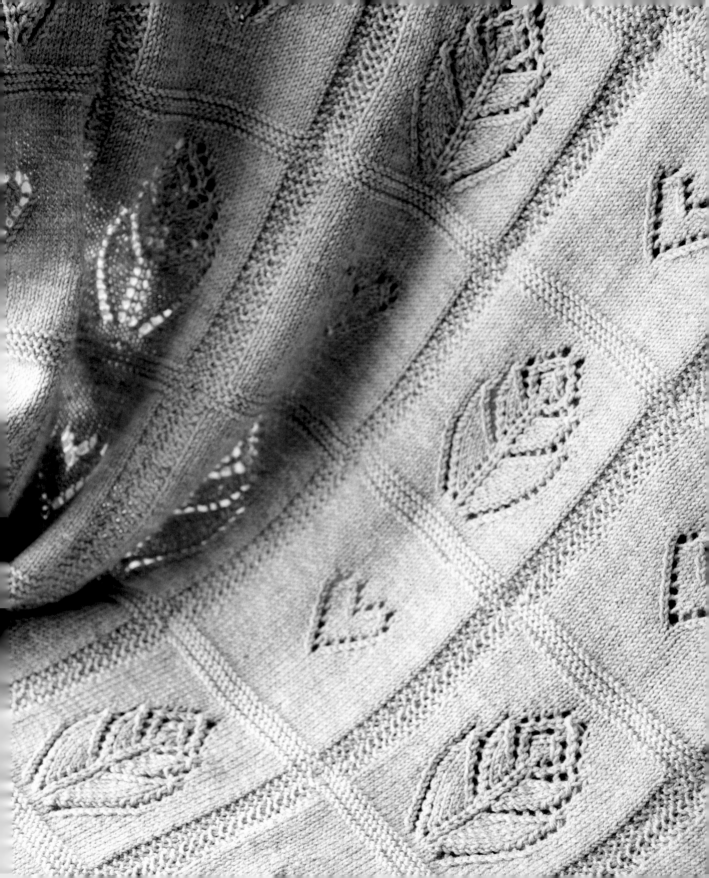

beach stripes blanket

This is knitted in four garter-stitch strips using three different designs, the first one being repeated for the fourth. Knitted in 9 different colourways of Rowan *Wool Cotton* or *Handknit Cotton*, its impact is gained from the different stripe combinations that make up each strip. Pattern on page 81.

beach stripes mat

Knitted in the same yarns as the Beach Stripes blanket (see page 36), this makes a great table or tea-tray mat – the perfect first colourwork project for a novice knitter. A narrow garter stitch edging makes a simple and attractive finishing touch. Pattern on page 84.

sunset cushion

A similarly two-tone textured design to the Simply Stripes cushion and blanket (see pages 14 and 16), this employs the Intarsia technique to create the central ridge and striped circle blocks, of which 9 are needed to make up the cushion. Knitted in Rowan *Pure Wool Superwash Worsted*. Pattern on page 86.

autumn leaves throw

Small stocking-stitch squares in 8 different colourways of Rowan *Felted Tweed* create the base for this rectangular throw to which 8 different garter-stitch leaf shapes, some striped, some plain, have been appliquéd. A similar leaf shape forms the trim, knitted in a ninth colour. The throw is 8 squares long by 4 squares wide. Pattern on page 88.

autumn leaves runner

A similar design to the throw on page 42 creates a little mat or runner, from a similar set of 8 squares and leaves in *Felted Tweed*, with or without a simple garter-stitch trim. The 8 blocks (right) indicate which leaf sits on which coloured square. Pattern on page 91.

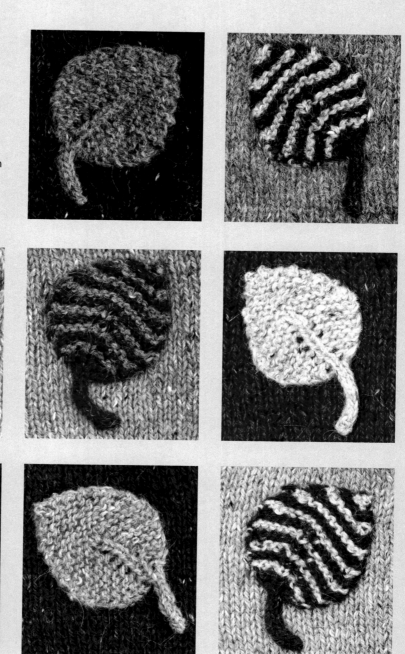

colour blocks blanket

YARN

Creative Focus Worsted

A	Nickel	00401	4 x 100gm
B	Marine	01660	1 x 100gm
C	Delft	01321	2 x 100gm
D	Teal	03360	3 x 100gm

OR

Pure Wool Superwash Worsted

A	Moonstone	112	4 x 100gm
B	Navy	149	1 x 100gm
C	Electric	143	2 x 100gm
D	Mallard	144	3 x 100gm

NEEDLES

1 pair 4.5 mm (US 7) needles

TENSION

20 sts and 24 rows to 10 cm (4 in) square measured over stocking stitch using 4.5 mm (US 7) needles, or size required to obtain correct tension.

FINISHED SIZE

Blanket measures approx 84 cm (33 in) x 108 cm (42½ in).

ABBREVIATIONS

See page 93.

BLANKET

BLOCK 1 [make 12]

Cast on 89 sts using 4.5mm (US 7) needles and yarn B.

Foundation row: K to end

Row 1 (RS): K2tog, [k19, k3tog] 3 times, k19, k2tog. *81sts*

Row 2 and every alt row: Knit.

Row 3: K2tog, [k17, k3tog] 3 times, k17, k2tog. *73sts*

Row 5: K2tog, [k15, k3tog] 3 times, k17, k2tog. *65sts*

Row 7: K2tog, [k13, k3tog] 3 times, k17, k2tog. *57sts*

Row 8: Knit.

Fasten off yarn B and join in yarn A. Now working in yarn A throughout cont working patt as set, working 2 less K sts between each decrease on every RS row until 9sts remain.

Next row: [k3tog] 3 times. *3sts*

Next row: K3tog and fasten off. Join seam to form a square.

BLOCK 2 [make 31]

Work as Block 1 using yarn A in place of yarn B (foundation row and next 8 rows), and yarn C in place of yarn A.

BLOCK 3 [make 20]

Work as Block 1 using yarn D throughout.

MAKING UP

Join blocks as shown on sketch, to form a large rectangle 7 blocks wide and 9 blocks long [63 blocks in total].

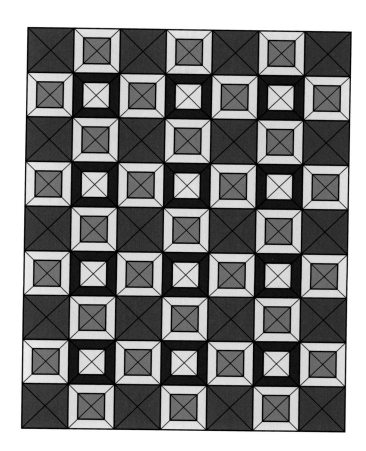

colour blocks cushion

YARN

Creative Focus Worsted

A	Nickel	00401	1 x 100gm
B	Basil	01350	1 x 100gm
C	Golden Heather	00018	1 x 100gm
D	New Fern	01265	1 x 100gm

OR

Pure Wool Superwash Worsted

A	Moonstone	112	1 x 100gm
B	Hawthorn	141	1 x 100gm
C	Rust	106	1 x 100gm
D	Olive	125	1 x 100gm

NEEDLES

1 pair 4.5 mm (US 7) needles

EXTRAS

35 cm (14 in) square cushion pad
39 cm (15½ in) square of backing fabric

TENSION

20 sts and 24 rows to 10 cm (4 in) square measured over stocking stitch using 4.5 mm (US 7) needles, or size required to obtain correct tension.

FINISHED SIZE

Cushion measures approx 35 cm x 35 cm (14 in x 14 in)

ABBREVIATIONS

See page 93.

CUSHION FRONT

BLOCK 1 [make 4]

Cast on 89 sts using 4.5mm (US 7) needles and yarn B.

Foundation row: K to end

Row 1 (RS): K2tog, [k19, k3tog] 3 times, k19, k2tog. *81sts*

Row 2 and every alt row: Knit.

Row 3: K2tog, [k17, k3tog] 3 times, k17, k2tog. *73sts*

Row 5: K2tog, [k15, k3tog] 3 times, k17, k2tog. *65sts*

Row 7: K2tog, [k13, k3tog] 3 times, k17, k2tog. *57sts*

Row 8: Knit.

Fasten off yarn B and join in yarn A. Now working in yarn A throughout cont working patt as set, working 2 less K sts between each decrease on every RS row until 9sts remain.

Next row: [k3tog] 3 times. *3sts*

Next row: K3tog and fasten off.

Join seam to form a square.

BLOCK 2 [make 4]

Work as Block 1 using yarn A in place of yarn B (foundation row and next 8 rows) and yarn C in place of yarn A

BLOCK 3 [make 1]

Work as Block 1 using yarn D throughout.

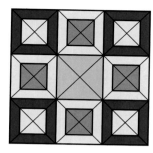

MAKING UP

To form Cushion front: Join blocks as shown on sketch, to form a large square 3 blocks wide and 3 blocks long [9 blocks in total]. Trim backing fabric to same size as knitted section, adding seam allowance along all edges. Fold 1 cm/½ in seam allowance to WS along all edges of backing fabric. Lay backing fabric onto knitted piece with WS facing and sew backing fabric in place along 3 sides. Insert cushion pad, then close 4th side.

creative cables throw

YARN

Pure Wool Superwash Worsted

A	Granite	111	2 x 100gm
B	Damson	150	2 x 100gm
C	Apple	129	3 x 100gm
D	Mallard	144	2 x 100gm
E	Oak	159	2 x 100gm
F	Soft Cream	102	2 x 100gm
G	Chestnut	107	3 x 100gm

OR

Pure Wool Superwash Worsted

A	Granite	111	2 x 100gm
B and G	Damson	150	5 x 100gm
C	Olive	125	3 x 100gm
D	Mallard	144	2 x 100gm
E	Rust	106	2 x 100gm
F	Soft Cream	102	2 x 100gm

NEEDLES

1 pair 4.5 mm (US 7) and 4 mm US 6) needles
1 cable needle

TENSION

19 sts and 25 rows to 10 cm (4 in) square measured over stocking stitch using 4.5 mm (US 7) needles, or size required to obtain correct tension.

FINISHED SIZE

Throw measures approx 115 cm (45½ in) x 150 cm (59 in)

ABBREVIATIONS

c4r = slip next st onto cable needle and hold at back of work, k3, then p1 from cable needle.

c4l = slip next 3 sts onto cable needle and hold at front of work, p1, then k3 from cable needle.

t4r = slip next st onto cable needle and hold at back of work, k3, then k1 from cable needle.

t4l = slip next 3 sts onto cable needle and hold at front of work, k1, then k3 from cable needle.

tw4r = slip next 2 sts onto cable needle and hold at back of work, k2, then p2 from cable needle.

tw4l = slip next 2 sts onto cable needle and hold at front of work, p2, then k2 from cable needle.

c5r = slip next 2 sts onto cable needle and hold at back of work, k3, then p2 from cable needle.

c5l = slip next 3 sts onto cable needle and hold at front of work, p2, then k3 from cable needle.

c4b[f] = slip next 2 sts on to a cable needle and hold in back [front] of work, k2 then k2 from cable needle.

c6b[f] = slip next 3 sts on to a cable needle and hold in back [front] of work, k3 then k3 from cable needle.

cr7b = slip next 4 sts on to a cable needle and hold in back of work, k3 then k4 from cable needle.

c8b = slip next 4 sts on to a cable needle and hold in back of work, k4 then k4 from cable needle

make bobble = [K1, p1, k1] all into next st, turn, p3, turn, k3, turn p3, turn sl1K, k2tog, psso.

See also page 93.

NOTE

When working from Charts, right side rows are read from right to left; wrong side rows are read from left to right.

THROW

CABLE STRIP 1

Cast on 38 sts using 4.5mm (US 7) needles and yarn A.

Cont to work from Chart 1, beg at bottom right hand corner [1st row is RS of work].

Work the 16 row patt rep 24 times, ending with RS facing for next row. *384 rows.*

Cast off.

CABLE STRIP 2

Cast on 45 sts using 4.5mm (US 7) needles and yarn B.

Cont to work from Chart 2, beg at bottom right hand corner [1st row is RS of work].

Work the 24 row patt rep 16 times, ending with RS facing for next row. *384 rows.*

Cast-off.

CABLE STRIP 3

Cast on 38 sts using 4.5mm (US 7) needles and yarn C.

Cont to work from Chart 3, beg at bottom right hand corner [1st row is RS of work].

Work the 12 row patt rep 32 times, ending with RS facing for next row. *384 rows.*

Cast-off.

CABLE STRIPS 1 AND 7

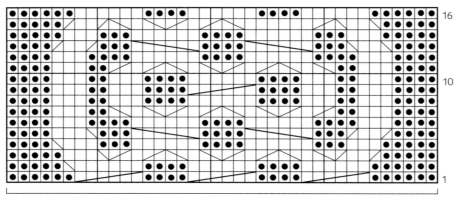

38 sts

CABLE STRIP 2

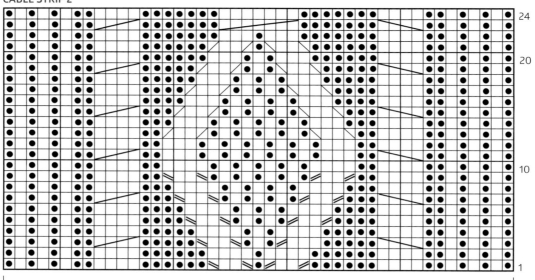

45 sts

CABLE STRIP 3

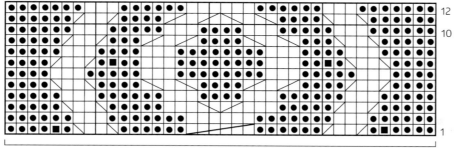

38 sts

CABLE STRIP 4

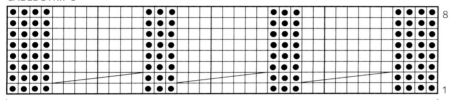

44 sts

CABLE STRIP 5

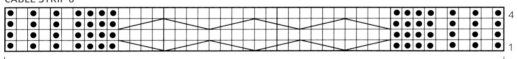

38 sts

CABLE STRIP 6

44 sts

KEY

☐ K on RS, P on WS

● P on RS, K on WS

⟋▢▢⟍ c4r

⟍▢▢⟍ c4l

⟍▢▢⟋ c4b

⟍▢▢⟍ c4f

▨▢▨ t4r

▨▢▨ t4l

⟋▢⟋ tw4r

⟍▢⟍ tw4l

⟋▢▢▢⟍ c5r

⟍▢▢▢⟍ c5l

▢▢▢▢⟋ c6b

⟍▢▢▢▢ c6f

▢▢▢▢▢▢⟋ cr7b

▢▢▢▢▢▢▢⟋ c8b

■ make bobble

CABLE STRIP 4

Cast on 44 sts using 4.5mm (US 7) needles and yarn D.
Cont to work from Chart 4, beg at bottom right hand corner [1st row is RS of work].
Work the 12 row patt rep 32 times, ending with RS facing for next row. *384 rows.*
Cast off.

CABLE STRIP 5

Cast on 38 sts using 4.5mm (US 7) needles and yarn E.
Cont to work from Chart 5, beg at bottom right hand corner [1st row is RS of work].
Work the 8 row patt rep 48 times, ending with RS facing for next row. *384 rows.*
Cast off.

CABLE STRIP 6

Cast on 44 sts using 4.5mm (US 7) needles and yarn F.
Cont to work from Chart 6, beg at bottom right hand corner [1st row is RS of work].
Work the 4 row patt rep 96 times, ending with RS facing for next row. *384 rows.*
Cast off.

CABLE STRIP 7

Cast on 38 sts using 4.5mm (US 7) needles and yarn G.
Cont to work from Chart of Cable Strip 1, beg at bottom right hand corner [1st row is RS of work].
Work the 16 row patt rep 24 times, ending with RS facing for next row. *384 rows.*
Cast off.

MAKING UP

Mattress stitch or slip stich all 7 strips neatly together as shown on sketch and in order to form one large rectangle.

SIDE EDGINGS [both alike]

Cast on 13 sts using 4mm (US 6) needles and yarn G.
Always twisting yarns together at right hand edge of work when changing colour and passing the darker colour over the lighter colour, cont in stripe garter stitch pattern as follows:-
Row 1 (RS): Using yarn C
Row 2: Using yarn C
Row 3: Using yarn G
Row 4: Using yarn G
These 4 rows form the stripe garter stitch pattern.
Cont to rep these 4 rows until work, when slightly stretched, fits up one entire row end edge of blanket and ending on a 3rd pattern row, WS facing for next row:-
Next row (WS): Using yarn G, cast off knitwise [on WS]
Repeat for opposite side edge.
Slip stitch or mattress stitch side edgings into place.

TOP EDGING

Cast on 13 sts using 4mm (US 6) needles and yarn G.
Cont in stripe garter stitch pattern until work, when slightly stretched, fits along entire top edge of blanket and across both short ends of side edgings and ending on a 3rd pattern row, WS facing for next row:-
Next row (WS): Using yarn G, cast off knitwise [on WS].
Slip stitch or mattress stitch top edging into place.

BOTTOM EDGING

Repeat as for top edging.

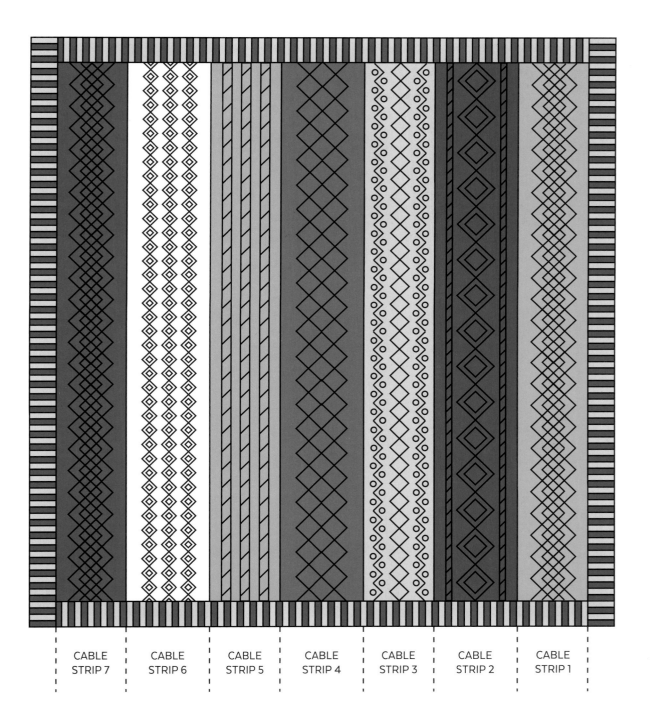

CABLE STRIP 7   CABLE STRIP 6   CABLE STRIP 5   CABLE STRIP 4   CABLE STRIP 3   CABLE STRIP 2   CABLE STRIP 1

simply stripes blanket and cushion

YARN

Felted Tweed

Blanket

A	Stone	190	4 x 50gm

Cushion

A	Stone	190	1 x 50gm

1 x 50gm of each of the following shades will be adequate to work both projects.

B	Ginger	154
C	Mineral	181
D	Maritime	167
E	Peony	183
F	Avocado	161
G	Seafarer	170
H	Bilberry	151
I	Pine	158
J	Seasalter	178
K	Rage	150
L	Treacle	145
M	Watery	152

NEEDLES

1 pair 3.75 mm (US 5) needles.

EXTRAS

Cushion only – 30 cm (12 in) x 40 cm (15½ in) cushion pad and 34cm (13½ in) x 44 cm (17½ in) rectangle of backing fabric.

TENSION

23 sts and 38 rows to 10 cm (4 in) measured over garter ridge stitch using 3.75 mm (US 5) needles, or size required to obtain correct tension.

FINISHED SIZE

Blanket measures approx 70 cm
(27½ in) x 90 cm (35½ in)
Cushion measures approx. 30 cm
(12 in) x 40 cm (15½ in)

ABBREVIATIONS

See page 93.

BLANKET

SQUARE 1 [make 9]

Cast on 23 sts using 3.75mm (US
5) needles and yarn A.

Row 1 (RS): Using yarn A Knit.

Row 2: Using yarn A Purl.

Row 3: Using yarn B Knit.

Row 4: Using yarn B Knit.

These 4 rows form the garter ridge
pattern.

Repeat these 4 rows 8 times more,
carrying colours not in use up side
of work.

Row 37 (RS): Using yarn A Knit.

Row 38: Using yarn A Purl.

Cast off knitwise.

SQUARES 2 TO 12

With A as the main [cast-on]
colour, make a further 54 blocks
as folls:-

Square 2 [make 6]: Repeat using
colours A and C

Square 3 [make 6]: Repeat using
colours A and D

Square 4 [make 6]: Repeat using
colours A and E

Square 5 [make 4]: Repeat using
colours A and F

Square 6 [make 4]: Repeat using
colours A and G

Square 7 [make 6]: Repeat using
colours A and H

Square 8 [make 4]: Repeat using
colours A and I

Square 9 [make 4]: Repeat using
colours A and J

Square 10 [make 6]: Repeat using
colours A and K

Square 11 [make 4]: Repeat using
colours A and L

Square 12 [make 4]: Repeat using
colours A and M

Total = 63 Squares

MAKING UP

Using back stitch or mattress stitch
if preferred, join all 63 squares
as shown by grid, to form a large
rectangle 7 squares wide and 9
squares long.

1	2	3	1	2	3	1
4	5	6	4	5	6	4
7	8	9	7	8	9	7
10	11	12	10	11	12	10
1	2	3	1	2	3	1
4	5	6	4	5	6	4
7	8	9	7	8	9	7
10	11	12	10	11	12	10
1	2	3	1	2	3	1

CUSHION

Work 1 square of each colourway as detailed on pages 00–00.
Total = 12 Squares

MAKING UP

Using back stitch or mattress stitch if preferred, join all 12 squares, as shown by grid, to form a large rectangle 3 squares wide and 4 squares long.
Trim backing fabric to same size as knitted section adding a seam allowance along all edges. Fold seam allowance to WS along all edges of backing fabric, Lay backing fabric onto knitted piece with WS facing and sew backing fabric in place along 3 sides. Insert cushion pad then close 4th side.

1	2	3
4	5	6
7	8	9
10	11	12

wintry blanket

YARN

Big Wool

Concrete   061   23 x 100gm

NEEDLES

1 pair 10 mm (US 15) needles
1 cable needle

TENSION

9 sts and 12.5 rows to 10 cm (4 in) measured over
stocking stitch using 10 mm (US 15) needles, or size
required to obtain correct tension.

FINISHED SIZE

Blanket measures approx 102 cm (40 in) x
230 cm (90½ in)

ABBREVIATIONS

c6b[f] = slip next 3 sts on to a cable needle and hold in
back [front] of work, k3 then k3 from cable needle
m1 = make one stitch by inserting needle from behind
under the running thread (which is the strand running
from the base of the stitch just worked to the base of
the next stitch) and lift this thread onto the left hand
needle, then knit one stitch into the back of it on RS,
purl one stitch into the back on WS.
See also page 93,

NOTE

When working from Charts, right side rows are read
from right to left; wrong side rows are read from left to
right.

THROW
CABLE STRIP 1

Cast on 38 sts using 10 mm (US 15) needles.

Row 1 (RS): (P1, K1) twice, P4, (K2, P2) 5 times, K2, P4, (K1, P1) twice.

Row 2: (K1, P1) twice, K4, P2, (K2, P2) 5 times, K4, (P1, K1) twice.

The last 2 rows sets the rib patt, rep the last 2 rows once more then row 1 again.

Row 6 (WS): (K1, P1) twice, K4, P2, K2, P2, K1, m1, K1, m1, P1, m1, P1, m1, K2, m1, P1, m1, P1, m1, K1, m1, K1, P2, K2, P2, K4, (P1, K1) twice. 46 sts.

Cont to work from Chart, beg at bottom right hand corner [1st row is RS of work].

Work the 8-row patt rep 38 times, then rows 1 to 7 once ending with WS facing for next row.

311 rows of chart worked.

Next row (WS): (K1, P1) twice, K4, P6, (p2tog) 4 times, P2, (p2tog) 4times, P6, K4, (P1, K1) twice. *38 sts.*

Work the rib patt as set for 6 rows ending with RS facing for next row.

Cast off in rib.

CABLE STRIP 2 (make 2)

Cast on 38 sts using 10 mm (US 15) needles

Row 1 (RS): (P1, K1) twice, P4, (K2, P2) 5 times, K2, P4, (K1, P1) twice.

Row 2: (K1, P1) twice, K4, P2, (K2, P2) 5 times, K4, (P1, K1) twice.

The last 2 rows sets the rib patt, rep the last 2 rows once more then row 1 again.

Row 6 (WS): (K1, P1) twice, K4, (P1, m1, P1, K1, m1, K1, P2, K1, m1, K1, P1, m1, P1, K2) twice, K2, (P1, K1) twice. *46 sts.*

CABLE STRIP 1

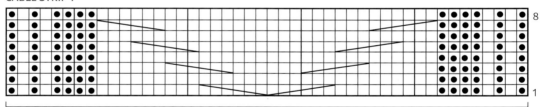

46 sts

CABLE STRIP 2

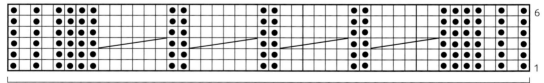

46 sts

KEY

 K on RS, P on WS

 P on RS, K on WS

  c6b

c6f

Cont to work from Chart, beg at bottom right hand corner [1st row is RS of work].

Work the 6-row patt rep 51 times, then rows 1 to 5 once ending with WS facing for next row.

311 rows of chart worked.

Next row (WS): (K1, P1) twice, K4, (p2tog, P1) twice, P2, (p2tog, P1) twice, K2, (P1, P2tog) twice, P2, (P1, P2tog) twice, K4, (P1, K1) twice.

38 sts.

Work the rib patt as set for 6 rows ending with RS facing for next row. Cast off in rib.

MAKING UP

Mattress stitch or slip stich the 3 strips neatly together with strip 1 at centre.

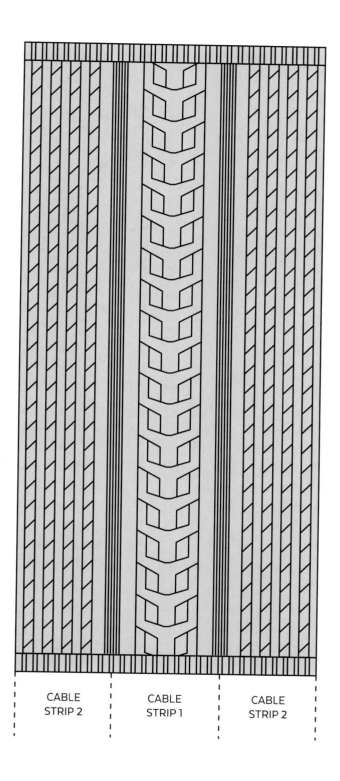

CABLE STRIP 2   CABLE STRIP 1   CABLE STRIP 2

winter trees cushion

YARN

Alpaca Colour

Marble	145	6 x 50gm
OR		

Felted Tweed

Stone	190	6 x 50gm
OR		

Pure Wool Superwash DK

Flint	105	6 x 50gm

NEEDLES

1 pair 4 mm (US 6) needles.

EXTRAS

50 cm (19½ in) square cushion pad.
90 x Debbie Abrahams size 6 Beads.

TENSION

22 sts and 30 rows to 10 cm (4 in) square measured over stocking stitch using 4 mm (US 6) needles, or size required to obtain correct tension.

FINISHED SIZE

Cushion measures approx 50 cm x 50 cm (19½ in x19½ in)

ABBREVIATIONS

See page 93.

Special Note for Beads

Place bead (on WS); place bead by taking yarn to RS of work, slipping bead up next to the stitch just worked, slip next stitch purlways from left needle to right needle and bring yarn back to WS, leaving bead sitting in front of slipped stitch.

NOTE

When working from Chart, right side rows are read from right to left; wrong side rows are read from left to right.

CUSHION FRONT

LACE TREE BLOCK 1 [make 5]

Cast on 37 sts using 4mm (US 6) needles.
Cont to work from chart, beg at bottom right hand corner (1st row is RS of work) until all 53 rows have been worked, ending with WS facing for next row.
Cast off knitwise.

TEXTURED TREE BLOCK 2 [make 4]

Cast on 37 sts using 4mm (US 6) needles.
Cont to work from chart, beg at bottom right hand corner (1st row is RS of work) until all 53 rows have been worked, ending with WS facing for next row.
Cast off knitwise

CUSHION BACK

Cast on 111 sts using 4mm (US 6).
Beg with a knit row, cont to work in stocking stitch throughout until work measures 50 cm (19½ in) from cast on edge, ending with RS facing for next row.
Cast off.

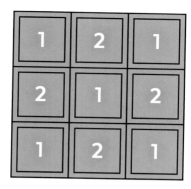

MAKING UP

To form Cushion front: Join blocks as shown in diagram to form a square 3 squares wide and 3 squares long [9 blocks in total] with the 'Lace Tree' block in each corner and at centre.

Attach both sides of cushion together using back stitch or mattress stitch if preferred along 3 sides. Insert cushion pad, then close 4th side.

LACE TREE BLOCK 1

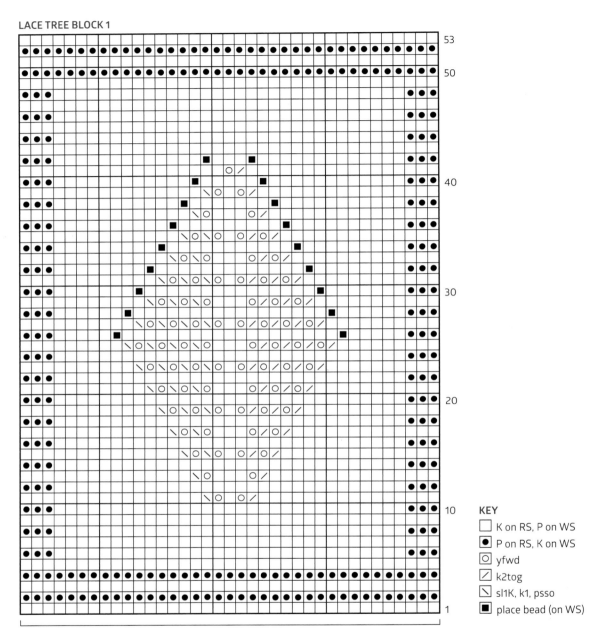

TEXTURED TREE BLOCK 2

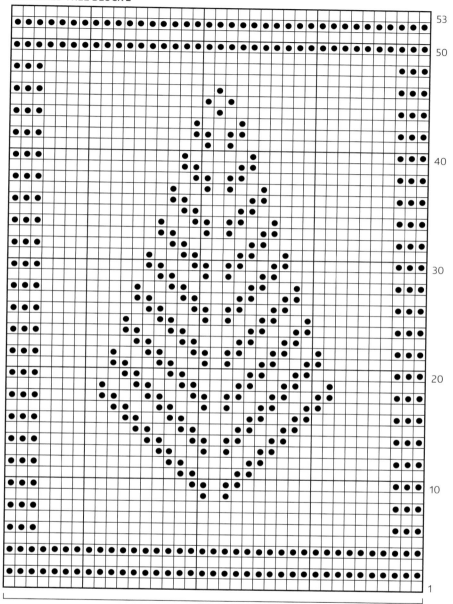

37 sts

little folk cushion

YARN

Wool Cotton 4 ply

A	Cloudy	505	3 x 50gm
B	Misty	496	2 x 50gm

OR

Summerlite 4 ply

A	Washed Linen	418	3 x 50gm
B	Pepper Pot	431	2 x 50gm

NEEDLES

1 pair 3.25 mm (US 3) [3 mm (US2/3) if using Summerlite 4ply] needles.
1 x 2.75mm (US 2) long circular needle.

EXTRAS

Cushion pad 35cm (14 in) square.
Backing fabric 39cm (15½ in) square.

TENSION

28 sts and 36 rows to 10 cm (4 in) square measured over stocking stitch using 3.25 mm (US 3) needles [3 mm (US 2/3) if using Summerlite 4ply], or size required to obtain correct tension.

FINISHED SIZE

Cushion measures approx 35 cm (14 in) x 35 cm (14 in)

ABBREVIATIONS

M1 = make one stitch by inserting needle from behind under the running thread (which is the strand running from the base of the stitch just worked to the base of the next stitch) and lift this thread onto left hand needle; then knit one stitch in to the back of it.
See also page 93.

NOTE

When working from Charts, right side rows are read from right to left; wrong side rows are read from left to right.

CUSHION FRONT

BLOCKS (make 1 of each of the 9 blocks)
Cast on 29 sts using 3.25mm (US 3) [3 mm (US 2/3) if using Summerlite 4 ply] needles and yarn A for blocks 1, 3, 5, 7 and 9 and yarn B for blocks 2, 4, 6 and 8.
Beg with a K row cont to work each chart entirely in stocking stitch using the Fairisle technique beg at bottom right hand corner (1st row is RS of work) until all 38 rows have been worked, ending with RS facing for next row.
Cast off.

MAKING UP

Using back stitch or mattress stitch if preferred, join all 9 blocks as shown by diagram, to form a square 3 blocks wide and 3 blocks long.
Trim backing fabric to same size as knitted front adding seam allowance along all edges. Fold seam allowances to WS along all edges of backing fabric. Lay backing fabric on to knitted piece with WS facing and sew in place along 3 sides. Insert cushion pad then close 4th side.

1	2	3
4	5	6
7	8	9

KEY
☐ Colour A
▨ Colour B

BLOCK 1

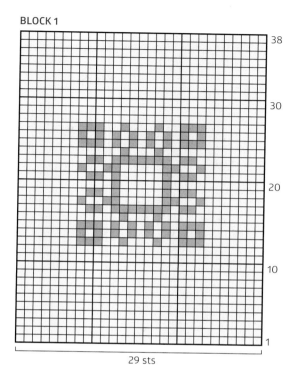

29 sts

BLOCK 2

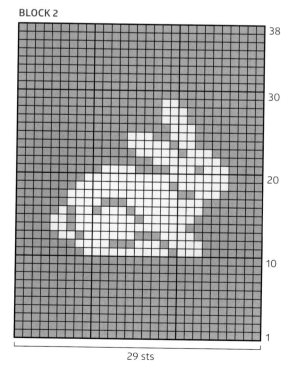

29 sts

BLOCK 3

BLOCK 5

BLOCK 4

BLOCK 6

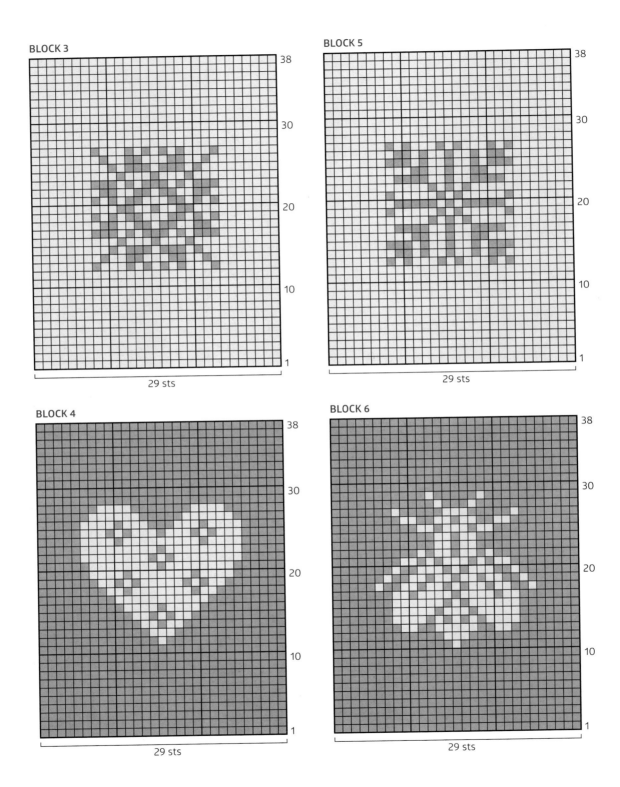

29 sts

BLOCK 7

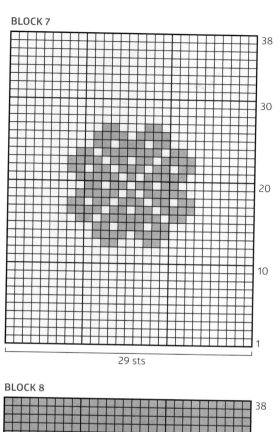

38

30

20

10

1

29 sts

BLOCK 9

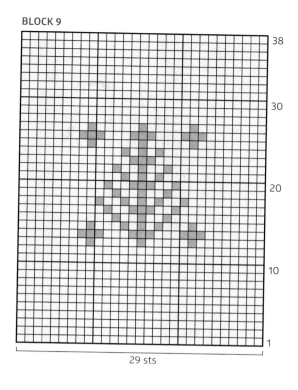

38

30

20

10

1

29 sts

BLOCK 8

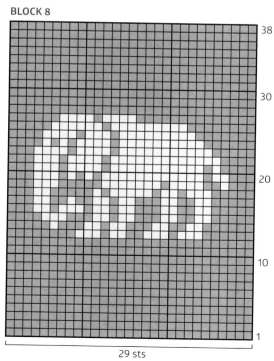

38

30

20

10

1

29 sts

KEY

☐ Colour A

▨ Colour B

little folk blanket

YARN

Wool Cotton 4 ply

A	Cloudy	505	3 x 50gm
B	Misty	496	2 x 50gm
C	Prune	506	1 x 50gm

OR

Summerlite 4 ply

A	Washed Linen	418	3 x 50gm
B	Pepper Pot	431	2 x 50gm
C	Aubergine	432	1 x 50gm

NEEDLES

1 pair 3.25 mm (US 3) [3 mm (US2/3) if using Summerlite 4ply] needles.
1 x 2.75mm (US 2) long circular needle.

TENSION

28 sts and 36 rows to 10 cm (4 in) square measured over stocking stitch using 3.25 mm (US 3) needles [3 mm (US 2/3) if using Summerlite 4ply], or size required to obtain correct tension.

FINISHED SIZE

Cot blanket measures approx 60 cm (23½ in) x 83 cm (32½ in)

ABBREVIATIONS

M1 = make one stitch by inserting needle from behind under the running thread (which is the strand running from the base of the stitch just worked to the base of the next stitch) and lift this thread onto left hand needle; then knit one stitch in to the back of it. See also page 93.

NOTE

When working from Charts, right side rows are read from right to left; wrong side rows are read from left to right.

COT BLANKET

BLOCK 1 (make 4)
Cast on 29 sts using 3.25mm (US 3) [3 mm (US 2/3) if using Summerlite 4 ply] needles and yarn A.
Beg with a K row cont to work Chart (see page 67) entirely in stocking stitch using the Fairisle technique beg at bottom right hand corner (1st row is RS of work) until all 38 rows have been worked, ending with RS facing for next row.
Cast off.

BLOCKS 2-9

Work the following Blocks as set by Block 1 from the relevant charts on pages 67–69, casting on using yarn A for blocks 3, 5, 7 and 9 and yarn B for blocks 2, 4, 6 and 8;
Block 2 [make 4]
Block 3 [make 2]
Block 4 [make 6]
Block 5 [make 6]
Block 6 [make 3]
Block 7 [make 4]
Block 8 [make 4]
Block 9 [make 2]
Total = 35 Blocks

MAKING UP

Using back stitch or mattress stitch if preferred, join all 35 blocks as shown by diagram opposite, to form a large rectangle 5 blocks wide and 7 blocks long.

TOP EDGING

With RS facing using 2.75mm (US 2) needles and yarn C pick up and K 180 sts evenly along cast-off edge of blanket.

Row 1 (WS): Knit.

Row 2: K1, m1, K to last st, m1, K1.

Rep the last 2 rows twice more. *186 sts.*

Cast off knitwise.

BOTTOM EDGING

With RS facing using 2.75mm (US 2) needles and yarn C pick up and K 180 sts evenly along cast-on edge of blanket.

Row 1 (WS): Knit.

Row 2: K1, m1, K to last st, m1, K1.

Rep the last 2 rows twice more. *186 sts.*

Cast off knitwise.

SIDE EDGINGS [both alike]

With RS facing using 2.75mm (US 2) needles and yarn C pick up and K 250 sts evenly along cast-on edge of blanket.

Row 1 (WS): Knit.

Row 2: K1, m1, k K to last st, m1, K1.

Rep the last 2 rows twice more. *256 sts.*

Cast off knitwise.

Join corners of all edgings.

modern art blanket

YARN

Pure Wool Worsted

A	Mustard	131	3 x 100gm
B	Umber	110	2 x 100gm
C	Oats	152	2 x 100gm
D	Rosy	115	2 x 100gm
E	Gold	133	1 x 100gm
F	Granite	111	1 x 100gm
G	Cocoa Bean	105	1 x 100gm

OR

Pure Wool Worsted

A	Olive	125	3 x 100gm
B	Damson	150	2 x 100gm
C	Mole	157	2 x 100gm
D	Rust	106	2 x 100gm
E	Gold	133	1 x 100gm
F	Granite	111	1 x 100gm
G	Hawthorn	141	1 x 100gm

OR

Pure Wool Worsted (Monochrome Colourway)

A	Moonstone	112	3 x 100gm
B	Black	109	2 x 100gm
C and G	Mole	157	3 x 100gm
D	Charcoal Grey	155	2 x 100gm
E	Almond	103	1 x 100gm
F	Granite	111	1 x 100gm

NEEDLES

1 pair 4 mm (US 6) needles.

TENSION

20 sts and 34 rows to 10 cm (4 in) square measured over garter stitch using 4 mm (US 6) needles, or required size to obtain correct tension.

FINISHED SIZE

Blanket measures approx 97.5 cm (38½ in) x 120 cm (47 in)

ABBREVIATIONS

See page 93.

BLANKET

STRIP 1

Cast on 39 sts using 4 mm (US 6) needles and yarn A. Cont in garter stitch as folls [ie. every row K]:-

190 rows using yarn A

76 rows using yarn B

189 rows using yarn C, ending with WS facing for next row.

Cast off knitwise [on WS].

STRIP 2

Cast on 39 sts using 4 mm (US 6) needles and yarn D. Cont in garter stitch as folls [ie. every row K]:-

228 rows using yarn D

38 rows using yarn E

189 rows using yarn D, ending with WS facing for next row.

Cast off knitwise [on WS].

STRIP 3

Cast on 39 sts using 4 mm (US 6) needles and yarn F. Cont in garter stitch as folls [ie. every row K]:-

152 rows using yarn F

76 rows using yarn A

38 rows using yarn G

189 rows using yarn A, ending with WS facing for next row.

Cast off knitwise [on WS].

STRIP 4

Cast on 39 sts using 4 mm (US 6) needles and yarn B.
Cont in garter stitch as folls [ie. every row K]:-
Work 455 rows using yarn B, ending with WS facing for next row.
Cast off knitwise [on WS].

STRIP 5

Cast on 39 sts using 4 mm (US 6) needles and yarn A.
Cont in garter stitch as folls [ie. every row K]:-
190 rows using yarn A
76 rows using yarn F
189 rows using yarn C, ending with WS facing for next row.
Cast off knitwise [on WS].

MAKING UP

Matching the garter ridge-rows of each strip and using a neat mattress stitch to join strips together, join all 5 strips together as shown in diagram.

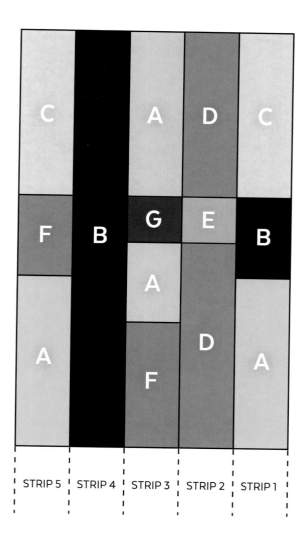

icelandic cushion

YARN

Felted Tweed Aran

A	Stoney	742	2 x 50gm
B	Mahogany	734	2 x 50gm

OR

Felted Tweed Aran

A	Scree	756	2 x 50gm
B	Carbon	759	2 x 50gm

NEEDLES

1 pair 4.5 mm (US 7) needles.

EXTRAS

50 cm (19½ in) square cushion pad
54 cm (21½ in) square of backing fabric

TENSION

16 sts and 23 rows to 10 cm (4 in) square measured over stocking stitch using 4.5 mm (US 7) needles, or size required to obtain correct tension.

FINISHED SIZE

Cushion measures approx 50 cm x 50 cm (19½ in x19½ in)

ABBREVIATIONS

See page 93.

NOTE

When working from Charts, right side rows are read from right to left; wrong side rows are read from left to right.

CUSHION FRONT

BLOCK 1 (make 5)

Cast on 31 sts using 4.5mm (US 7) needles and yarn B. Cont to work from Chart beg at bottom right hand corner (1st row is RS of work), working in st st throughout and using the Fairisle technique until all 31 rows have been worked, ending with WS facing for next row.
Cast off knitwise.

BLOCK 2 (make 2)

Cast on 31 sts using 4.5mm (US 7) needles and yarn A. Work as Block 1.

BLOCK 3 (make 2)

Cast on 31 sts using 4.5mm (US 7) needles and yarn A. Work as Block 1.

BLOCK 1

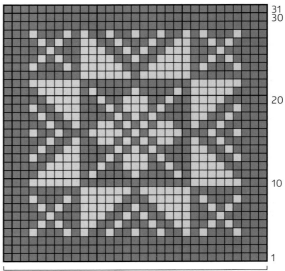

31 sts

MAKING UP

To form Cushion front: Join blocks as shown on diagram, to form a square 3 blocks wide and 3 blocks long [9 blocks in total].

Trim backing fabric to same size as knitted section, adding seam allowance along all edges. Fold seam allowance to WS along all edges of backing fabric. Lay backing fabric onto knitted piece with WS facing and sew backing fabric in place along 3 sides. Insert cushion pad, then close 4th side.

1	**2**	**1**
3	**1**	**3**
1	**2**	**1**

KEY

☐ Colour A
■ Colour B

BLOCK 2

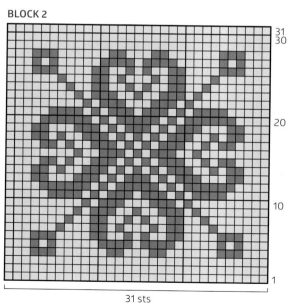

31 sts

BLOCK 3

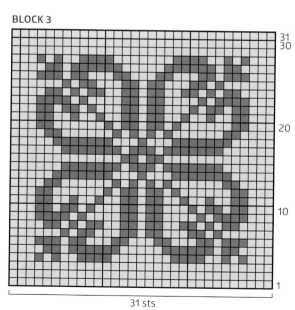

31 sts

springtime blanket

YARN

Superfine Merino 4 ply

Marble   269   11 x 50gm

NEEDLES

1 pair 3.25 mm (US 3) needles.

TENSION

28 sts and 36 rows to 10 cm (4 in) square measured over stocking stitch using 3.25 mm (US 3) needles, or size required to obtain correct tension.

FINISHED SIZE

Blanket measures approx 87 cm (34½ in) x 112 cm (44 in)

ABBREVIATIONS

See page 93.

NOTE

When working from Charts, right side rows are read from right to left; wrong side rows are read from left to right.

BLANKET

BLOCK 1 [make 32]

Cast on 33 sts using 3.25mm (US 3) needles.

Cont to work from Chart on page 78 beg at bottom right hand corner (1st row is RS of work) until all 49 rows have been worked, ending with WS facing for next row.
Cast off knitwise.

BLOCK 2 [make 31]

Cast on 33 sts using 3.25mm (US 3) needles.

Cont to work from Chart on page 79 beg at bottom right hand corner (1st row is RS of work) until all 49 rows have been worked, ending with WS facing for next row.
Cast off knitwise.

MAKING UP

Using back stitch or mattress stitch if preferred, join all 63 squares as shown by diagram, to form a large rectangle 7 blocks wide and 9 blocks long.

1	2	1	2	1	2	1
2	1	2	1	2	1	2
1	2	1	2	1	2	1
2	1	2	1	2	1	2
1	2	1	2	1	2	1
2	1	2	1	2	1	2
1	2	1	2	1	2	1
2	1	2	1	2	1	2
1	2	1	2	1	2	1

BLOCK 1

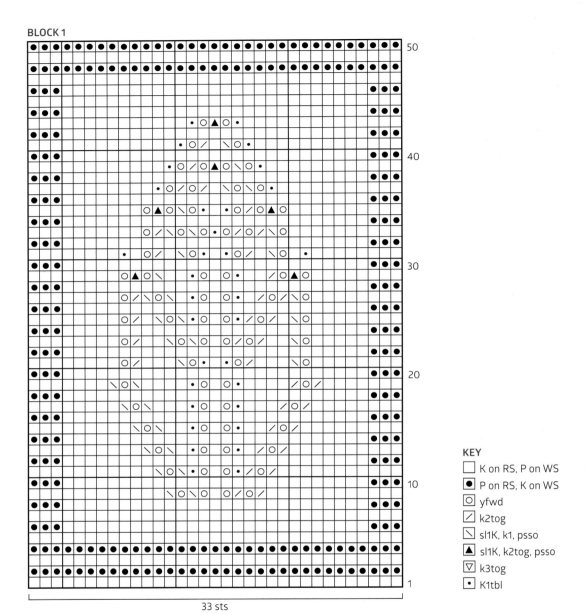

33 sts

KEY

☐	K on RS, P on WS
●	P on RS, K on WS
○	yfwd
╱	k2tog
╲	sl1K, k1, psso
▲	sl1K, k2tog, psso
▽	k3tog
•	K1tbl

BLOCK 2

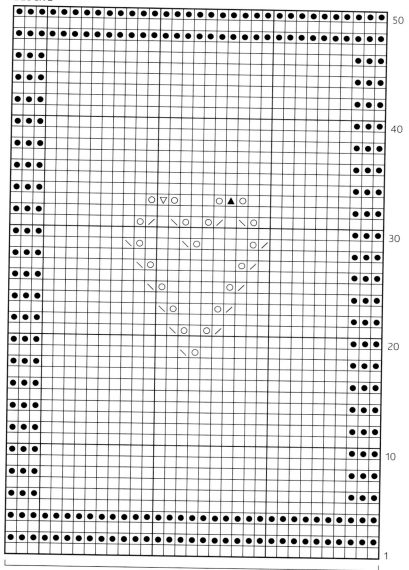

springtime cushion

YARN

Summerlite 4 ply

Washed Linen   418   3 x 50gm

NEEDLES

1 pair 3 mm (US 2/3) needles.

EXTRAS

Cushion pad 35 cm (14 in) square.

TENSION

28 sts and 36 rows to 10 cm (4 in) square measured over stocking stitch using 3 mm (US 2/3) needles, or size required to obtain correct tension.

FINISHED SIZE

Cushion measures approx 35 cm (14 in) x 35 cm (14 in)

ABBREVIATIONS

See page 93.

NOTE

When working from Charts, right side rows are read from right to left; wrong side rows are read from left to right.

CUSHION FRONT

BLOCK 1 [make 5]

Cast on 33 sts using 3mm (US 2/3) needles.
Cont to work from Chart on page 78 beg at bottom right hand corner (1st row is RS of work) until all 49 rows have been worked, ending with WS facing for next row.
Cast off knitwise.

BLOCK 2 [make 4]

Cast on 33 sts using 3mm (US 2/3) needles.
Cont to work from Chart on page 79 beg at bottom right hand corner (1st row is RS of work) until all 49 rows have been worked, ending with WS facing for next row.
Cast off knitwise.

CUSHION BACK

Cast on 99 sts using 3mm (US 2/3) needles.
Beg with a knit row cont in stocking stitch until work measures 35cm (14 in), ending with RS facing for next row.
Cast off.

MAKING UP

To form Cushion Front:- Join blocks as shown on photograph to form a square 3 blocks wide and 3 blocks long [9 blocks in total] with block 1 in each corner and at centre.

Attach both sides of cushion together using back stitch or mattress stitch if preferred, along 3 sides. Insert cushion pad, then close 4th side.

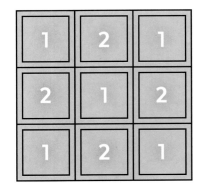

beach stripes blanket

YARN

Wool Cotton

A	Rich	911	2 x 50gm
B	Moss Gray	990	2 x 50gm
C	Elf	946	2 x 50gm
D	Lichen	922	2 x 50gm
E	Antique	900	2 x 50gm
F	Larkspur	988	2 x 50gm
G	Misty	903	1 x 50gm
H	Inky	908	2 x 50gm
I	Pier	983	1 x 50gm

OR

Handknit Cotton

A	Rosso	215	2 x 50gm
B	Linen	205	2 x 50gm
C	Gooseberry	219	2 x 50gm
D	Forest	370	2 x 50gm
E	Ecru	251	2 x 50gm
F	Thunder	335	2 x 50gm
G	Slate	347	1 x 50gm
H	Black	252	2 x 50gm
I	Atlantic	346	1 x 50gm

NEEDLES
1 pair 3.25 mm (US 3) needles

1 x 3.25 mm (US 3) long circular needle

TENSION
23 sts and 46 rows to 10 cm (4 in) square measured over garter stitch using 3.25 mm (US 3) needles, or required size to obtain correct tension.

FINISHED SIZE
Blanket measures approx 70 cm (27½ in) x 116 cm (45½ in)

ABBREVIATIONS
See page 93.

BLANKET
STRIP 1 [make 2]

Cast on 31 sts using 3.25mm (US 3) needles and yarn A.

Cont in garter stitch as folls [ie. every row K]:-

Work 4 rows using yarn A [for lower border]

Cont in garter stitch work the following stripe sequence 5 times:-

18 rows using yarn B

6 rows using yarn C

6 rows using yarn D

18 rows using yarn E

6 rows using yarn C

18 rows using yarn D

6 rows using yarn B

18 rows using yarn C

6 rows using yarn A

510 rows of stripe sequence worked.

Knit 18 rows using yarn B.

Knit 5 rows using yarn A, WS facing for next row:-

Next row (WS): Using yarn A cast off knitwise [on WS – the last 6 rows form top border].

STRIP 2 [make 2]

Cast on 31 sts using 3.25mm (US 3) needles and yarn A.

Cont in garter stitch as folls [ie. every row K]:-

Work 4 rows using yarn A [for lower border]

Cont in garter stitch work the following stripe sequence 5 times:-

18 rows using yarn F

6 rows using yarn G

6 rows using yarn H

6 rows using yarn E

6 rows using yarn H

18 rows using yarn I
6 rows using yarn H
6 rows using yarn C
18 rows using yarn G
6 rows using yarn E
6 rows using yarn H
510 rows of stripe sequence worked.
Knit 18 rows using yarn F.
Knit 5 rows using yarn A, WS facing for next row:-
Next row (WS): Using yarn A cast off knitwise [on WS – the last 6 rows form top border]

STRIP 3 [make 1]
Cast on 31 sts using 3.25mm (US 3) needles and yarn A.
Cont in garter stitch as folls [ie. every row K]:-
Work 4 rows using yarn A [for lower border].
Cont in garter stitch work the following stripe sequence 5 times:-
18 rows using yarn G
6 rows using yarn H
18 rows using yarn E
6 rows using yarn G
6 rows using yarn A
6 rows using yarn G
18 rows using yarn E
6 rows using yarn H
6 rows using yarn F
6 rows using yarn H
6 rows using yarn F
510 rows of stripe sequence worked.
Knit 18 rows using yarn G.
Knit 5 rows using yarn A, WS facing for next row:-

Next row (WS): Using yarn A cast off knitwise
[on WS – the last 6 rows form top border].

MAKING UP

Matching the garter ridge-rows of each strip and using a neat mattress stitch to join strips together, join all 5 strips as shown in illustration.

SIDE EDGINGS [both alike]

With RS facing using 3.25mm (US 3) circular needle and yarn A, pick up and knit 265 sts along row end edge of blanket.
Knit 4 rows ending with WS facing for next row.
Next row (WS): Cast off knitwise

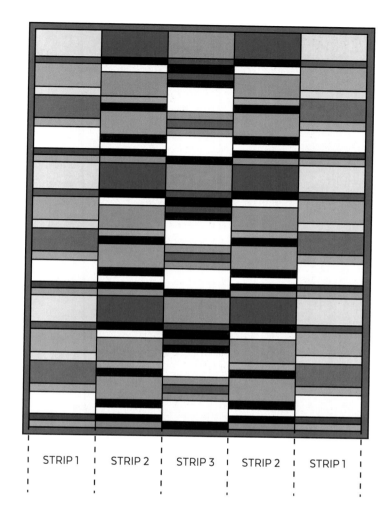

STRIP 1 STRIP 2 STRIP 3 STRIP 2 STRIP 1

beach stripes mat

YARN

Wool Cotton

A	Rich	911	1 x 50gm
B	Moss Gray	990	1 x 50gm
C	Elf	946	1 x 50gm
D	Lichen	922	1 x 50gm
E	Antique	900	1 x 50gm
F	Larkspur	988	1 x 50gm
G	Misty	903	1 x 50gm
H	Inky	908	1 x 50gm
I	Pier	983	1 x 50gm

OR

Handknit Cotton

A	Rosso	215	1 x 50gm
B	Linen	205	1 x 50gm
C	Gooseberry	219	1 x 50gm
D	Forest	370	1 x 50gm
E	Ecru	251	1 x 50gm
F	Thunder	335	1 x 50gm
G	Slate	347	1 x 50gm
H	Black	252	1 x 50gm
I	Atlantic	346	1 x 50gm

NEEDLES

1 pair 3.25 mm (US 3) needles

TENSION

23 sts and 46 rows to 10 cm (4 in) square measured over garter stitch using 3.25 mm (US 3) needles, or required size to obtain correct tension.

FINISHED SIZE

Mat measures approx 36 cm (14 in) x 29 cm (11½ in)

ABBREVIATIONS

See page 93.

MAT

STRIP 1

Cast on 25 sts using 3.25mm (US 3) needles and yarn A.

Cont in garter stitch as folls [ie. every row K]:-

4 rows using yarn A [for lower border]

18 rows using yarn B

6 rows using yarn C

6 rows using yarn D

18 rows using yarn E

6 rows using yarn C

18 rows using yarn D

6 rows using yarn B

18 rows using yarn C

6 rows using yarn A

18 rows using yarn B

5 rows using yarn A ending with WS facing for next row:-

Next row (WS): Using yarn A cast off knitwise [on WS - the last 6 rows form top border].

STRIP 2

Cast on 25 sts using 3.25mm (US 3) needles and yarn A.

Cont in garter stitch as folls [ie. every row K]:-

4 rows using yarn A [for lower border]

18 rows using yarn F

6 rows using yarn G

6 rows using yarn H

6 rows using yarn E

6 rows using yarn H

18 rows using yarn I

6 rows using yarn H

6 rows using yarn C

18 rows using yarn G

6 rows using yarn E

6 rows using yarn H

18 rows using yarn F

5 rows using yarn A ending with WS facing for next row:-

Next row (WS): Using yarn A cast off knitwise [on WS – the last 6 rows form top border].

STRIP 3

Cast on 25 sts using 3.25mm (US 3) needles and yarn A.

Cont in garter stitch as folls [ie. every row K]:-

4 rows using yarn A [for lower border]

18 rows using yarn G

6 rows using yarn H

18 rows using yarn E

6 rows using yarn G

6 rows using yarn A

6 rows using yarn G

18 rows using yarn E

6 rows using yarn H

6 rows using yarn F

6 rows using yarn H

6 rows using yarn F

8 rows using yarn G

5 rows using yarn A ending with WS facing for next row:-

Next row (WS): Using yarn A cast off knitwise [on WS – the last 6 rows form top border].

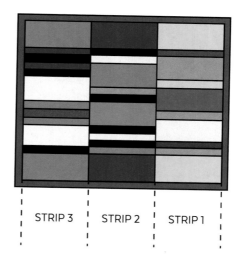

STRIP 3   STRIP 2   STRIP 1

MAKING UP

Matching the garter ridge-rows of each strip and using a neat mattress stitch to join strips together, join all 3 strips as shown in illustration.

SIDE EDGINGS [both alike]

With RS facing using 3.25mm (US 3) needles and yarn A, pick up and Knit 70 sts along row end edge of mat.

Knit 4 rows ending with WS facing for next row.

Next row (WS): Cast off knitwise.

sunset cushion

YARN

Pure Wool Superwash Worsted

A	Charcoal Grey	155	2 x 100gm
B	Light Denim	154	2 x 100gm

OR

Pure Wool Superwash Worsted

A	Charcoal Grey	155	2 x 100gm
B	Moonstone	112	2 x 100gm

NEEDLES

1 pair 4.5 mm (US 7) needles.

EXTRAS

45 cm (17½ in) square cushion pad.

TENSION

20 sts and 25 rows to 10 cm (4 in) square measured over stocking stitch using 4.5 mm (US 7) needles, or size required to obtain correct tension.

FINISHED SIZE

Cushion measures approx 45 cm x 45 cm (17½ in x17½ in)

ABBREVIATIONS

See page 93.

NOTE

When working from Chart, right side rows are read from right to left; wrong side rows are read from left to right.

CUSHION FRONT

BLOCK 1 [make 5]

Cast on 30 sts using 4.5mm (US 7) needles and yarn A. Cont to work from chart, beg at bottom right hand corner (1st row is RS of work) until all 47 rows have been worked changing colours when necessary and working the contrast areas of the circle using the Intarsia technique (i.e. use a separate ball/length of yarn for each block of colour, twisting yarns together at WS of work when changing colour), ending with WS facing for next row.

Cast off knitwise.

BLOCK 2 [make 4]

Cast on 30sts using 4.5mm (US 7) needles and yarn B. Work as Block 1 using colours as stated on key for block 2.

CUSHION BACK

Cast on 89 sts using 4.5mm (US 7) needles and yarn A. Working in garter st throughtout (i.e. knit every row). Work the foll 4 row stripe sequence:-

Row 1 and 2: Using yarn A.

Row 3 and 4: Using yarn B.

Cont as set until cushion back meas 45cm (17½ in) ending with WS facing for next row.

Cast off knitwise.

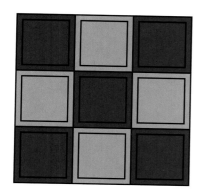

MAKING UP

To form Cushion front: Join blocks as shown in diagram to form a square 3 blocks wide and 3 blocks long [9 blocks in total] with block 1 in each corner and at centre. Attach both sides of cushion together using back stitch or mattress stitch if preferred, along 3 sides. Insert cushion pad, then close 4th side.

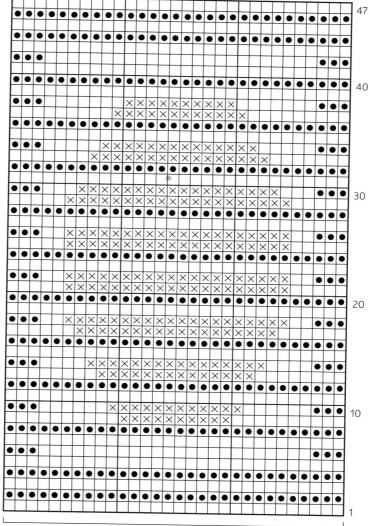

30 sts

KEY

	Block 1: K on RS, P on WS in A Block 2: K on RS, P on WS in B
●	Block 1: P on RS, K on WS in A Block 2: P on RS, K on WS in B
✕	Block 1: K on RS, P on WS in B Block 2: K on RS, P on WS in A

autumn leaves throw and runner

YARN

Felted Tweed

1 x 50gm of each of the following shades will be adequate to work both projects.

A	Mineral	181
B	Tawny	186
C	Camel	157
D	Phantom	153
E	Ginger	154
F	Avocado	161
G	Pine	158
H	Clay	177

(Used for the chair back only)

I	Peony	183	2 x 50gm

NEEDLES

1 pair 3.75 mm (US 5) needles and 2.75 mm (US 2) needles.

2 x 2.75 mm (US 2) double pointed needles.

TENSION

24 sts and 32 rows to 10 cm (4 in) square measured over stocking stitch using 3.75 mm (US 5) needles, or size required to obtain correct tension.

FINISHED SIZE

Sofa throw without trim measures approx 40 cm (15½ in) x 80 cm (31½ in)

Runner measures approx. 20 cm (8 in) x 40 cm (15½ in)

ABBREVIATIONS

See page 93.

SOFA THROW

SQUARES

Make 4 squares in yarns A, B, C, D, E, F, G and H as folls:-

Cast on 24 sts using 3.75mm (US 5) needles.

Work 32 rows in stocking stitch (i.e – knit RS rows and purl WS rows), ending with RS facing for next row.

Cast off.

Total = 32 squares

LEAF 1 (make 4)

Cast on 3 sts using 2.75 mm (US 2) double pointed needles and yarn G.

Stalk

Row 1 (RS): K3, *without turning work slip these 3 sts to opposite end of needle and bring yarn to opposite end of work pulling it quite tightly across back of these 3 sts. Using the other needle K these 3 sts again; rep from * 7 times more.

Main Leaf

Change to normal 2.75 mm (US 2) needles.

Row 1 (RS): K1, yfwd, K1, yfwd, K1, using yarn G. *5 sts.*

Row 2: K2, P1, K2, using yarn G.

When changing colours carry up the side of the work taking the darker shade over the lighter colour.

Row 3: K2, yfwd, K1, yfwd, K2, using yarn H. *7 sts.*

Row 4: K3, P1, K3 using yarn H.

Row 5: K3, yfwd, K1, yfwd, K3, using yarn G. *9 sts.*

Row 6: K4, P1, K4 using yarn G.

Row 7: K4, yfwd, K1, yfwd, K4, using yarn H. *11 sts.*

Row 8: K5, P1, K5 using yarn H.

Row 9: K5, yfwd, K1, yfwd, K5, using yarn G. *13 sts.*

Row 10: K6, P1, K6 using yarn G.

Row 11: K6, yfwd, K1, yfwd, K6, using yarn H. *15 sts.*

Row 12: K7, P1, K7 using yarn H.

Row 13: K7, yfwd, K1, yfwd, K7, using yarn G. *17 sts.*

Row 14: K8, P1, K8 using yarn G.

Row 15: ssk, K to last 2 sts, k2tog, using yarn H. *15 sts.*

Row 16: K to end using yarn H.

Row 17: ssk, K to last 2 sts, k2tog, using yarn G. *13 sts.*

Row 18: K to end using yarn G.

Row 19: ssk, K to last 2 sts, k2tog, using yarn H. *11 sts.*

Row 20: K to end using yarn H.

Row 21: ssk, K to last 2 sts, k2tog, using yarn G. *9 sts.*

Row 22: K to end using yarn G.

Row 23: ssk, K to last 2sts, k2tog, using yarn H. *7 sts.*

Row 24: K to end using yarn H.

Row 25: ssk, K to last 2 sts, k2tog, using yarn G. *5 sts.*

Row 26: K to end using yarn G.

Row 27: ssk, K to last 2 sts, k2tog, using yarn H. *3 sts.*

Row 28: K to end using yarn H.

Row 29: K3tog and fasten off.

LEAVES 2-8

Make 4 each of the following leaves as set by Leaf 1 and swopping colours as stated below;

Leaf 2: Use yarn A throughout.

Leaf 3: Replace yarn G with yarn B and yarn H with yarn F.

Leaf 4: Use yarn F throughout.

Leaf 5: Use yarn H throughout.

Leaf 6: Replace yarn G with yarn D and yarn H with yarn A.

Leaf 7: Use yarn C throughout.

Leaf 8: Replace yarn G with yarn E and yarn H with yarn C.

Total = 32 Leaves

MAKING UP

Sew leaves to top of corresponding square (i.e leaf 1 with square 1). Squares 1–4 with 'tip' of leaf pointing to bottom right hand corner of square, bending 'stalk' slightly to the right. Remaining squares 5–8, with 'tip' of leaf pointing to bottom left hand corner of square, bending 'stalk' slightly to the left.

Using back stitch or mattress stitch if preferred, join all 32 squares as shown by diagram, to form a large rectangle 4 squares wide and 8 squares long.

TRIM

Cast on 8 sts using 2.75 mm (US 2) needles and yarn I.

Row 1 (RS): K5, yfwd, K1, yfwd, K2.

Row 2: P6, inc in next st by knitting into front and back of it, K3.

Row 3: K4, P1, K2, yfwd, K1, yfwd, K3.

Row 4: P8, inc in next st, K4.

Row 5: K4, P2, K3, yfwd, K1, yfwd, K4.

Row 6: P10, inc in next st, K5.

Row 7: K4, P3, K4, yfwd, K1, yfwd, K5.

Row 8: P12, inc in next st, P6.

Row 9: K4, P4, sl1K, K1, psso, K7, k2tog, K1.

Row 10: P10, inc in next st, K7.

Row 11: K4, P5, sl1K, K1, psso, K5, k2tog, K1.

Row 12: P8, inc in next st, K2, P1, K5.

Row 13: K4, P1, K1, P4, sl1K, K1, psso, K3, k2tog, K1.

Row 14: P6, inc in next st, K3, P1, K5.

Row 15: K4, P1, K1, P5, sl1K, K1, psso, K1, k2tog, K1.

Row 16: P4, inc in next st, K4, P1, K5.

Row 17: K4, P1, K1, P6, sl1K, k2tog, psso, K1.

Row 18: P2tog, cast-off 5 sts using the p2tog as the first of these sts (1 st on right hand needle), K1, P1, K5.

These 18 rows form the trim patt.

Cont to repeat these 18 rows until the trim fits around entire outer edge of chair back, slip stitching straight edge of trim into place as you go along, slightly gathering the trim at the corners and ending after a full pattern repeat.

Cast off. Join cast-on and cast-off edges together.

1	2	3	4
5	6	7	8
1	2	3	4
5	6	7	8
1	2	3	4
5	6	7	8
1	2	3	4
5	6	7	8

KOREA
My Knit Studio, 3F, 144 Gwanhun-Dong, 110-300 Jongno-Gu, Seoul
Tel: 82-2-722-0006 Email: myknit@myknit.com
Web: www.myknit.com

LATVIA
Coats Latvija SIA, Mukusalas str. 41 b, Riga LV-1004
Tel: +371 67 625173   Fax: +371 67 892758
Email: info.latvia@coats.com Web: www.coatscrafts.lv

LEBANON
y.knot, Saifi Village, Mkhalissiya Street 162, Beirut
Tel: (961) 1 992211 Fax: (961) 1 315553 Email: y.knot@cyberia.net.lb

LITHUANIA and RUSSIA
MEZ Crafts Lithuania UAB, A. Juozapaviciaus str. 6/2,
LT-09310 Vilnius
Tel: +370 527 30971   Fax: +370 527 2305
Email: info.lt@mezcrafts.com Web: www.coatscrafts.lt

LUXEMBOURG
Coats N.V., c/o Coats GmbH, Kaiserstr.1, 79341 Kenzingen, Germany
Tel: 00 49 7644 802 222 Fax: 00 49 7644 802 133
Email: sales.coatsninove@coats.com Web: www.coatscrafts.be

MEXICO
Estambres Crochet SA de CV, Aaron Saenz 1891-7Pte, 64650
MONTERREY
Tel: +52 (81) 8335-3870 Email: abremer@redmundial.com.mx

NEW ZEALAND
ACS New Zealand, P.O Box 76199, Northwood, Christchurch
Tel: 64 3 323 6665 Fax: 64 3 323 6660 Email: lynn@impactmg.
co.nz

NORWAY
Carl J. Permin A/S Egegaardsvej 28 DK-2610 Rødovre
Tel: (45) 36 72 12 00 E-mail: permin@permin.dk

PORTUGAL
Mez Crafts Portugal, Lda – Av. Vasco da Gama, 774-4431-059 V.N,
Gaia
Tel: 00 351 223 770700 Email: sales.iberia@mezcrafts.com

SINGAPORE
Golden Dragon Store, BLK 203 Henderson Rd #07-02, 159546
Henderson Indurstrial Park
Tel: (65) 62753517 Fax: (65) 62767112 Email: gdscraft@hotmail.
com

SLOVAKIA
MEZ Crafts Slovakia, s.r.o. Seberíniho 1, 821 03 Bratislava
Tel: +421 2 32 30 31 19 Email: galanteria@mezcrafts.com

SOUTH AFRICA
Arthur Bales LTD, 62 4th Avenue, Linden 2195
Tel: (27) 11 888 2401 Fax: (27) 11 782 6137
Email: arthurb@new.co.za
Web: www.arthurbales.co.za

SPAIN
MEZ Fabra Spain S.A, Avda Meridiana 350, pta 13 D,
08027 Barcelona
Tel: +34 932908400 Fax: +34 932908409
Email: atencion.clientes@mezcrafts.com

SWEDEN
Carl J. Permin A/S Egegaardsvej 28 DK-2610 Rødovre
Tel: (45) 36 72 12 00 Email: permin@permin.dk

SWITZERLAND
MEZ Crafts Switzerland GmbH, Stroppelstrasse20,
5417 Untersiggenthal
Tel: +41 00800 2627 2800 Fax: 0049 7644 802 133
Email: verkauf.ch@mezcrafts.com Web: www.mezcrafts.ch

TURKEY
MEZ Crafts Tekstil A.S, Kavacık Mahallesi, Ekinciler Cad. Necip Fazıl
Sok.
No.8 Kat: 5, 34810 Beykoz/İstanbul
Tel: +90 216 425 88 10 Web: www.mezcrafts.com

TAIWAN
Cactus Quality Co Ltd, 7FL-2, No. 140, Sec.2 Roosevelt Rd, Taipei,
10084 Taiwan, R.O.C.
Tel: 00886-2-23656527 Fax: 886-2-23656503
Email: cqcl@ms17.hinet.net

THAILAND
Global Wide Trading, 10 Lad Prao Soi 88, Bangkok 10310
Tel: 00 662 933 9019 Fax: 00 662 933 9110
Email: global.wide@yahoo.com

U.S.A.
Westminster Fibers, 8 Shelter Drive, Greer, South Carolina, 29650
Tel: (800) 445-9276 Fax: 864-879-9432
Email: info@westminsterfibers.com

U.K
Coats Crafts UK, Green Lane Mill, Holmfirth, West Yorkshire,
England HD9 2DX
Tel: +44 (0) 1484 681881 Fax: +44 (0) 1484 687920
Email: ccuk.sales@coats.com Web: www.knitrowan.com

For more stockists in all countries please visit www.rowan.com

YARNS

The following Rowan yarns have been used in this book:

Alpaca Colour
Alpaca: 100%; 50g balls; 120m/131yd per ball; 22 sts and 30 rows over 10cm/4in using 4mm (US 6) needles.

Big Wool
100% Merino wool; 100g balls; 80m/87yd per ball; 7½-9sts and 10-12½ rows over 10cm/4in using 10 or 15mm (US 15-19) needles.

Creative Focus Worsted
75% wool; 25% alpaca;100g balls; 200m/220yd per ball; 20sts and 24 rows to 10cm/4in using 4.5mm (US 7) needles.

Felted Tweed
Merino Wool: 50%; Alpaca: 25%; Viscose: 25%; 50g balls; 175m/191yd per ball; 22-24sts and 30-32 rows to 10cm/4in using 3.75-4mm (US 5-6) needles.

Felted Tweed Aran
Merino Wool: 50%, Alpaca: 25%, Viscose: 25%;50g balls; 87m/95yd per ball;16sts and 23 rows to 10cm/4in using 5mm (US 8) needles.

Hemp Tweed
Wool: 75%; True Hemp: 25%; 50g balls; 95m/104yd per ball; 19sts and 25 rows to 10cm/4in using 4.5mm (US 7) needles.

Pure Wool DK
100 per cent Superwash Wool; 50g balls; 130m/142yd per ball; 22sts and 30 rows to 10cm/4in using 4mm (US size 6) needles.

Pure Wool Superwash Worsted
Superwash Wool: 100%; 100g balls; 200m/219yd per ball; 20 sts and 25 rows over 10cm/4in using 4.5mm (US 7) needles.

Summerlite 4 ply
Cotton: 100%: 50g balls; 175m/191yd per ball; 28 sts and 36 rows over 10cm/4in using 3mm (US 2-3) needles.

Superfine Merino 4 ply
Merino wool: 100%; 50g balls; 165m (181yd) per ball; 28 sts and 36 rows over 10cm/4in using 3.25mm (US 3) needles.

Superwash Wool 100%
100g balls; 200m/219yd per ball; 20sts and 25rows to 10cm/4in using 4.5mm (US 7) needles.

Wool Cotton
Cotton: 50%, Merino Wool: 50per cent 50g balls; 113m/124yd per ball; 22-24 sts and 30-32 rows over 10cm/4in using 3.75-4mm (US 5-6) needles.

Wool Cotton 4 ply
Cotton: 50%, Merino Wool: 50%; 50g balls; 180m/197yd per ball; 28 sts and 36 rows over 10cm/4in using 3.25mm (US 3) needles.